B D S M
O
O
K

MW01167534

100 Creative BDSM Punishments

- Ideas for dominant men and dominant women -

Dom. Ination

Foreword

Hello dear reader. It doesn't matter if you bought this book yourself, or if it was given to you by your sub. It will serve its purpose. Of course, not all 100 ideas will match your preferences, but you will certainly find something. And maybe the suggestion will also awaken your ideas and you will find one or the other punishment for your sub yourself.

My name is Dom. Ination. Of course it's a synonym. And since it doesn't matter whether I'm male, female, dominant or submissive, I won't go into detail here either. After all, this book is not about me. It is about you! It's about your submissive! And it's about how you manage to make your sessions or even the small punishments for misconduct by your sub more exciting.

I have been interested in BDSM for over 10 years now and since I find punishments that everyone else does boring and uncreative, I have collected good, unusual and exciting ideas over a long period of time and put them together for this book. Because to my knowledge there are few such offerings on the market and it is something I myself would like to have in my BDSM repertoire. But since the offers that were made for it didn't appeal to me, I decided to simply implement it myself. And now you will benefit from it.

It's also important to remember that this is a punishment for your sub, not a reward (you can use my ideas as rewards, of course). But as punishment, you should choose something that your sub doesn't like and that he or she will be reluctant to do. Because otherwise it is not a punishment. But ALWAYS think about the taboos of your sub! A punishment must NEVER affect the taboos of your sub! The taboos are ABSOLUTE and should not even be scratched! You MUST know where the limits are and what you can and are allowed to do! As the dominant part in the relationship, you are responsible for the well-being of your submissive! And in the end, it's about both having fun doing it. Both you and your sub. While you want to punish your sub for wrongdoing, you should never overdo it.

If any of the punishments are falling under your subs preferences, just dare to incorporate it into your sessions if you feel like it. Or maybe you use it as a reward rather than a punishment. You have no limits. Feel free to be creative. It will be so much more fun and different for you and your sub.

But now enough of the words from me. Here are the hundred ideas for punishing your sub.

I would also appreciate if you write a review and let me know how the book has helped you and whether there were many punishments that you will implement with your sub.

But now have fun on your discovery tour.

Punishment 1

Take a normal rubber band. The color does not matter. If you have a prefered color of course you can use it. Pull the rubber band over your submissives fingers so that it ends before the thumb and encloses the palm and back oft he hand.

This can be used during a session and does not interfere in any way. If the sub is misbehaving and you want to hit him or her, you simply pull the rubber band and let it bounce back. It's uncomfortable, but nothing bad can happen. Therefore, this punishment is very suitable for beginners, but even experienced subs will be surprised if you use this method because they are certainly not familiar with it.

You need: Rubber bands

Punishment 2

Your sub is shy and you want to punish him or her for an offense with something that makes him or her uncomfortable? Have him or her sing something for you or write a poem and recite it to you.

This is a severe punishment for someone who doesn't like doing this in front of others at all. Of course it will be very entertaining for you to watch your or your sub and you can sit back, relax and enjoy it.

You need: You do not need any tools for this punishment. Except maybe something to write about if you want your sub to write the poem down as well.

Punishment 3

Grab a handful of dried peas. Yes, you heard that right, peas. Put them in your or your sub's socks. Now let her or him walk in front of you, dance, fidget as if it were a catwalk. Without, of course, letting him or her say anything. If you didn't like it, just have your sub start the performance all over again. Do this until you are really satisfied.

You need: For this punishment you need dried peas.

Punishment 4

Do you include punishments in everyday life? Just let your sub wear your underwear for a day. Would you like her to walk around in your Batman boxer shorts? Or him in your pink thong or your sexy hot pants?

Of course, this punishment is much more humiliating for male subs than for females. But of course it's not a punishment if he's into feminization and maybe even your sissy.

You need: Your worn or unworn underwear in which you would like to see your sub.

Punishment 5

You are into pee games, but it's not your sub's preference? (Of course it can't be taboo!) Why not have a drink together in the evening while you get cozy. You might even light a candle to put yourself in a good mood.

In your glass you have cola, wine, water, sparkling wine, juice, ... whatever tastes particularly good to you. Of course he or she has your urine in the glass. To make it particularly interesting and special, you can use real wine glasses. Then the candles and maybe you let your sub cook a great dinner.

Now you can toast and... cheers. You'll enjoy watching your sub drain the glass while you enjoy your own drink. Do you maybe even refill your subs glass?

You need: Two glasses, your drink and your urine. Possibly things like candles, music, ... be imaginative.

Punishment 6

If it's something for you and your sub, why not just ban him or her from wearing clothes all day? Naked posture can be used very well as a punishment. It doesn't matter whether it's cooking, cleaning, watching TV, ... today your sub is naked. The whole time.

For you it will be eye candy and for your sub it will be humiliating to have to be naked all day while you are clothed. Take every opportunity to touch your sub if you feel like it and use him or her for your sexual desires in between.

Please remember that it should be warm enough. After all, you don't want your sub to catch a cold.

You need: You do not need any tools for this penalty.

Punishment 7

Why don't you be a little mean to your sub if you want to punish him or her? How about if you eat something and then there is a delicious dessert? Maybe even your sub's favorite dessert?

However, the dessert is only for you. Your sub has to watch you eat the whole dessert with relish and in front of his or her eyes.

Be sure to let him or her know how delicious it tastes, so this will make the punishment even worse for your sub.

You need: After the meal, you need your sub's favorite dessert. However, only one portion for you.

Punishment 8

Your sub was naughty? Just let him or her eat on the floor while you sit at the table. Was he or she really cheeky? Then just let him or her eat naked. Are you really mad at your sub? Then he or she can just eat from a bowl. Of course without cutlery. If you don't have a bowl, you can put a soup plate in front of your sub.

It will clearly show your sub the power imbalance between you and demean him or her to behave better in the future.

You need: A bowl. Alternatively, you can use a soup plate.

Punishment 9

Another very good way to punish a sub is by simply ignoring him or her. Do you do this for an hour? Maybe a whole day?

Of course, you can also forbid him or her to speak unsolicited. Do this for a while and it will be a very long and unbearable time for your submissive.

You need: You do not need any tools for this punishment.

Punishment 10

Have your sub stand against the wall with their hands behind their backs and their noses pressing a piece of paper, a coin, or something similar against the wall. It's best to tie your sub's hands behind his or her back so he or she doesn't get the idea of cheating.

The item must not fall, of course, and the longer it takes, the more Sub will have to concentrate to keep the item in place.

If you feel like it, you can also torment him or her with a crop, your hands, a whip or similar during this time. This will make it all the more difficult for your sub to complete his or her task and not drop the item.

But please be careful not to hurt your sub if you hit him or her while he or she is standing so close to the wall. If you're not absolutely sure, don't hit them during this punishment.

You need: An object to be held against the wall with its nose. Possibly shackles and something to torment.

Punishment 11

A similar idea to not being allowed to sit at the table is if the sub is not allowed to sit on the couch when watching TV together. Have him or her kneel on the floor next to or in front of the couch while you get really comfortable.

If you want, you can also have your sub massage your feet. Or you slide to the edge and let your sub lick you or give you a blowjob while watching the TV.

However, don't let him or her on the couch until you're comfortable with the punishment. Your sub will certainly learn to behave better as a result.

You need: For this punishment you need nothing more than your living room.

Punishment 12

Of course we don't want to forget one of the classics. An orgasm ban for your sub. But normally it would be boring. Why not just let him or her roll the dice for how many days he or she needs to stay chaste? If you're nice, it's just a cube. But of course you can also be mean and there are 2, 3 or more dice and the eyes are added together. Or are the eyes of the dice even multiplied together?

With this punishment you let your sub seal his or her fate themself.

You need: For this punishment you need one or more dice.

Punishment 13

If your sub has been naughty, why not do some exercise as punishment for him or her? This is not necessarily fun for him or her, but it is definitely healthy and also ensures better physical well-being. So this punishment also has a positive effect on the sub.

You can also enjoy watching him or her do push-ups and more. Let him or her struggle a bit. Make the size of the penalty dependent on the size of the offense you want to punish.

Of course, you can also let your sub do the exercises naked, so that the sight is more delightful for you.

You need: You do not need any tools for this penalty.

Punishment 14

Have your sub wear a butt plug for a day. He or she will surely have to think about you and his or her offense all the time. For example, depending on how bad the offense was, you can control the intensity of the penalty by changing the size of the plug. There is a small plug for a small offense. If there's a big offense, there's a big plug.

But don't forget that wearing a plug for a long time can also lead to sores. I would therefore recommend a plug made of a softer material such as silicone, which your sub can then wear longer. If your sub doesn't have that much experience with it, you can do it for a shorter time.

After all, you don't want your sub to get sores and you might not be able to "play" for a long time.

But I think you know best what your sub can take and I'm just mentioning it again as a cautionary tale.

You need: For this punishment you need one or more anal plugs.

Punishment 15

You want to punish your sub for too many contradictions? How about a gag for this? If you don't have a gag, other things are also suitable, such as a scarf, tape (please be careful with male subs who have a beard. Tape is not necessarily recommended) or your worn underwear.

Problem solved. Now your sub is calm and there are no contradictions for a moment.

You need: A gag or alternatively something else that can serve as a substitute.

Punishment 16

Take a regular lock and leave it open. Fill a mold halfway with water and freeze it. When the water is frozen, take the key from the lock, place it in the center and fill the rest of the mold with water. Once frozen, the key will be inaccessible in the middle of the block of ice.

Now comes the interesting part. You can now lock something with the lock. It can be anything. A chastity belt, handcuffs, a box in which your sub's mobile phone is located or maybe you have a good idea yourself what you would like to lock.

Now you put the ice cube in a bowl and your sub has to wait until the ice has melted before revealing the key.

You need: A lock with a key, a bowl, water and a chest freezer or freezer. And of course something you want to close.

Punishment 17

Another and quite exciting way to punish a sub can be toys with radio remote controls. It doesn't matter if you use it at home in your own four walls, or if you let your sub wear it to the cinema, to a restaurant, to the theater, while shopping, ... it will be great fun for you.

Your sub never knows when you're going to vibrate it. Maybe while you're at the checkout to pay? While you order your food at the restaurant?

There are also toys that can give off small surges of electricity if you like something a little more extreme.

You need: A toy that you can control with a radio remote control or an app.

Punishment 18

Welcome back to school. Have your sub write a one- or multi-page essay about his or her behavior. In this way, it is easier to remember that he or she has behaved incorrectly.

Have him or her handwrite this essay to make it even more reminiscent of school and detention.

You need: Paper and a pen.

Punishment 19

If you're comfortable with the public seeing what your relationship is like, you can make your sub wear clothes that say their status as punishment.

There is actually almost everything on the internet. From the t-shirt that says 'Slut' to 'Sklave', 'Slave', 'Chastity Slave', 'Locked',... Just find something that you and your sub love and that suits you. Let Sub wear it when you go out together.

You need: A piece of clothing that has your sub's status written on it.

Punishment 20

A good way of punishing a sub is a forced orgasm. It is the exact opposite of an orgasm ban, as you bring the sub to the climax again and again. This eventually becomes very uncomfortable for the sub's penis or the sub's vagina. After a while it's just too oversensitive that the stimuli become a sweet agony.

You need: Either your hands, your tongue or sex toys to bring your sub to orgasm.

Punishment 21

Tie up your sub and then bring another person into the room to have sex with in front of your sub. Of course, it is important that you know that you can go this far, as you can also hurt your sub emotionally.

So you should already have discussed this topic in detail or already have experience with partner swapping, group sex or similar if you want to use something like this to punish your sub.

You need: Something to tie up your sub and someone to have sex with in front of your sub.

Punishment 22

You can also lend him or her to another dominant person to punish your sub. Of course, it is also important here that you know that you can do this with your sub. The most important thing, however, is that you are absolutely certain that the other dominant person, especially if you are not present to check, is only doing exactly what you have given permission for and what has been discussed in advance. After all, it's your sub and you're just lending him or her. Nevertheless, you are of course responsible for your sub. Remember that the taboos and limits of your sub must not be exceeded.

You need: Another dominant person to lend your sub to play with.

Punishment 23

A very nice and humiliating idea is to fuck the sub near the window. Preferably in such a way that you can see that he or she is a slave, sub, ... With a collar, maybe also tied up or take the male sub with a strap-on, for example.

Do you like the idea of flaunting your sub like this? But keep in mind that you have to be sure that you can do this with your sub.

You need: You do not need anything for this punishment, unless you would like to use something.

Punishment 24

Temporary tattoos that are washable are a beautiful and humiliating way to mark and demean your sub.

If you search the internet, you will find what you are looking for and also discover a lot related to BDSM. From the Triskele to Cum Slut, Fuck Toy, Fuck me, Anal Slut, Slave, Cuckold, Property of ..., ... there is almost everything you can think of.

And the good thing is, the tattoo is only there for a few days and if you really need to remove it, you can get it right off with a little scrubbing.

Should it be visible to the public, such as a small triskelion on the slave's neck? Or should it rather be hidden so that only you can see it when your sub is naked?

You need: For this punishment you need temporary tattoos that you can apply to your sub.

Punishment 25

To punish your sub, you can also make him or her wear clothing of the opposite sex. Your male sub in a dress is sure to be a fun sight for you. Or your female sub, sure looks ridiculous in your oversized clothes.

Whether you only do this at home or also in public depends on your inclinations and the taboos of your slave.

You need: An outfit of the opposite sex to tuck your sub into.

Punishment 26

Have your sub kneel on an uncomfortable surface and contemplate his or her offense. Dried peas, rice or similar are suitable, for example. Of course, things like marbles also work if you still have some.

Just be careful not to let your sub kneel on anything where he or she could actually hurt themselves. Always remember, you are responsible!

You need: For this punishment you need something for your sub to kneel on, which makes kneeling uncomfortable.

Punishment 27

Why not do a bit of acrobatics? Have your sub take an awkward position, balance on one leg, or something like that, and watch as he or she struggles to accomplish the task.

Feel free to point out mistakes to him or her and if you're not happy, just have your sub do it all over again.

You can also set up an hourglass in front of your sub and tell him or her that he or she made it when the sand on one side is completely gone. If you want to be mean, just flip the hourglass just before the sand runs through, extending the sub's punishment.

You need: For this punishment, it is advisable to use an hourglass and place it in the sub's field of vision.

Punishment 28

As punishment, you can also display your sub naked in one of your windows so that he or she can be seen in public. Unless, of course, it's one of your sub's taboos.

If you want, you can also threaten him or her that this will happen more often if he or she doesn't learn how to behave.

You need: For this punishment you actually only need a window that faces the street.

Punishment 29

Play a little Cinderella. It doesn't necessarily have to be peas and lentils. Maybe you have something else. The main thing is that you can throw different things together that your sub then has to sort out again.

Either way, you can keep your sub occupied for quite a while this way. Also, maybe ban something until he or she is done with the work. Favorite series? Soccer? All this is only available when the sorting is finished.

You need: For this punishment you will need two or more different types of small objects that you can throw together for your sub to then sort through.

Punishment 30

Do you have a favorite movie that your sub doesn't like at all? Look the movie as punishment. A very nice movie night for you and a long one for your sub.

Your sub will be glad when the movie is over. To add to the agony, you can now ask him or her questions about the film and see if he or she was paying attention.

If the answers are good, then everything is fine. However, if you are not satisfied, you should watch the film one more time. If it's already too late that evening, then maybe it's the program for the next evening?

You need: For this punishment you need a TV or computer and a movie that you like but your sub doesn't.

Punishment 31

Lie in bed naked. Your sub must turn on their side and not face you. Now you start masturbating yourself. Don't do this quietly and feel free to let your sub know how unfortunate it is that he or she is not allowed to participate because he or she must be punished. This will be very frustrating for your sub.

Of course, it is also important that your sub is not allowed to touch or satisfy himself! It's supposed to be punishment after all. And of course, even after you had a climax, there is none for your submissive today.

You need: You don't need anything for this punishment, unless you use sex toys to masturbate, then you need these.

Punishment 32

Are you a bit artistic today? Take a piece of ginger and carve a small butt plug out of it. It should be about finger size.

When this ginger dildo/plug is inserted anally, the ginger releases essential oils that induce a searing pain that is completely harmless, despite the intensity.

Your sub will certainly not like this punishment. It's important to remember that when you carve, you're creating a shape that has a part that prevents the plug from completely disappearing into the anus. You eventually want to be able to remove it.

Should you decide after punishment that your sub deserves an orgasm, then he or she will find that it will be much more intense due to the ginger sensitization.

You need: For this punishment you need a piece of ginger and something to peel and carve it into shape.

Punishment 33

What is your attitude towards tickle torture? Never tried it? Then you should definitely do it. Especially if your sub is ticklish.

This torture method dates back to the Middle Ages. There it was mainly used for surveys. Of course, it is very important that your sub is completely fixed and cannot move. So he or she has to endure the tickle torture. It can be tickled anywhere, but of course it is also possible on the genitals. Just try out where it is most effective on your sub. Maybe under their feet or on their stomach? Among the poor? And maybe you should experiment a little with pens, brushes and fingers to find out what works best on your sub.

You need: For this punishment you need restraints for your sub and possibly things like feathers and brushes to tickle him or her with.

Punishment 34

Rimming is a demeaning way of punishing the sub. Rimming is the stimulation of the anus with the tongue. If it's not taboo for your sub, it's a very nice and effective punishment that the dom can thoroughly enjoy, since there are a lot of nerve endings at the anus.

For the sub it is of course very humiliating to kiss the buttocks of the dom and to lick the anus.

To make it more intense and humiliating, you can also fix your sub and do it in the form of facesitting.

But please deal with this topic beforehand and inform yourself. Also you should clean your anus thoroughly beforehand.

You need: You don't need anything for this punishment. But it is advisable to invest some time beforehand and to deal more closely with the topic of rimming.

Punishment 35

How about a real classic of BDSM punishment? Electrostimulation. But normally it would be boring. With harmless but very intense electrical impulses, E-Stim Toys push the nerve tracts, the brain and thus also the pleasure centers of the sub's body to the limit.

In order to make the whole thing even more intense for the sub, you can also tie up his or her freedom of movement. And maybe a blindfold too, so Sub doesn't know where to you will shock them next?

A very nice toy for this are, for example, e-stim nipple clamps. They are suitable for punishing both male and female subs.

You need: For this punishment you need e-stim toys. You may need something to tie up your sub and blindfold his or her eyes.

Punishment 36

A very humiliating and therefore extremely effective punishment for a sub is objectification. Sub becomes a piece of furniture.

Your sub was naughty? You had a busy day? Have your sub undress and kneel in front of as a footstool. You don't like a stool? Then maybe a table or a drink holder?

To make the whole thing even more intense, you can also tie your sub into the desired shape. And maybe you gag your sub too. After all, a piece of furniture doesn't speak!

You need: You generally do not need any tools for this punishment, unless you prefer to use shackles.

Punishment 37

Let your sub get creative and give him or her the task of making you cum without using their hands or mouth (handling a dildo or sex toy obviously doesn't count!)

Now you can enjoy watching how your sub will try to fulfill this task.

You need: You do not need any tools for this punishment.

Punishment 38

Housework is never a nice thing. Just let your sub do the housework as punishment. And to make it a bit sexy you can have your sub clean naked. Or would you rather see your sub in lingerie?

Anyway, it will be a great sight for you. And the positive thing is, when Sub gets his or her punishment done, the chores get done at the same time. And if everything has been done properly and to your satisfaction, you might even get the idea that Sub might now deserve a reward. Or if you are dissatisfied with the result, then there is the next penalty. Of course, after your sub has had to finish the housework properly.

You need: For this punishment you generally do not need any special tools that you do not have in the household anyway.

Punishment 39

Do you have time the whole weekend? Sub is guilty of something you want to punish? How about letting Sub live blindfolded for a day? That could be very interesting for you and an intense experience for your sub.

You can also give him or her tasks. Recognizing objects by touch, for example. Or that he or she then has to spoil you blindly.

You need: For this punishment you only need a blindfold.

Punishment 40

Your sub got you really upset? Exhibitionism is not taboo, but also not a preference of your sub? Then take your sub for a little jaunt. He or she is your naked passenger. Of course you can also tie and gag him or her if you like.

And now you decide where to go. On the country road or maybe in the city where there are more people and someone will surely notice when you drive past like this?

You need: For this punishment you need a car and a driver's license.

Punishment 41

For a full day, your sub may not get up from a crawling or kneeling position as punishment. Of course, a weekend is best for this. Of course, you can also let your sub be naked to make it more entertaining for yourself. Of course, your sub has to move around that day as well.

You need: You do not need any tools for this punishment.

Punishment 42

Ice cube torture is also a nice way to punish a sub. It can be very uncomfortable when an ice cube slides over sensitive parts of the body.

Command your sub to remain still or tie him or her up directly so he or she cannot move. Now you can use ice cubes to find the sensitive parts of your sub's body. Does he react particularly strongly when the ice cube touches his testicles, penis or glans? Or does she react particularly strongly when you slide the ice cube along her vagina, maybe even press it on her clitoris?

If you want to increase the sensations of your sub, it is advisable to blindfold him or her. In this way, he or she perceives it even more intensely.

You need: For this punishment you need ice cubes. You may also need restraints and a blindfold if you want to use that.

Punishment 43

Sub was naughty? So punishment is necessary. Tie him or her up and put headphones on him or her. Now you play one and the same song on a loop. It's best if it's a song that your sub doesn't like.

You need: Something to tie your sub to, headphones and a song your sub doesn't like.

Punishment 44

Pointless and boring tasks can be excellent punishments. Have your sub move peas, lentils, grains of rice, ... individually from one container to another. Or something like putting in and clearing out a cupboard compartment again and again. The main thing is that it is a frustrating and pointless task. Your sub will hate this punishment. Feel free to be creative in your choice of meaningless task.

You need: In general, you do not need any special tools for this punishment.

Punishment 45

You can punish your sub by not letting him or her sleep in bed. If you're really nice, he or she gets the couch in the living room. Or would you rather let sub sleep in a sleeping bag or with a blanket next to the bed? Maybe you also have a cage where your sub can spend the night.

You need: You do not need any tools for this punishment.

Punishment 46

Playing with the cold can of course also be played with heat. Now you're probably thinking of candles, but I'll tell you something else great. Use a heat cream like Finalgon. Smear a bit of this on your sub's penis or vagina and watch him or her squirm. I promise it's a very nasty punishment that your sub won't soon forget.

You need: For this punishment you need a heat cream such as Finalgon.

Punishment 47

In winter, when there is snow, your sub can make a snow angel for you. But of course he or she has to do it naked. Or you can just let your sub be naked in the cold for a moment while you watch him or her do it.

You need: Since you cannot influence the weather, this punishment is only possible when there is snow.

Punishment 48

Ask your sub to make their own whip or flogger. Of course, he or she has to make an effort, since this percussion instrument is to be used often from now on. Maybe you give him or her a design that you particularly like.

This punishment will keep your sub busy for a while, but in the end you'll have a very personal and (hopefully) beautiful instrument of torture that you can then use to work on the sub with.

You need: If you would like to be so kind, you can get materials for your sub and make them available. But you can also let Sub do everything.

Punishment 49

You aren't shy? Then go to a swinger party with your sub. Here you have a lot of options. Either you sleep with others in front of her or his eyes, while he or she is only allowed to watch without taking any action themself. Another possibility is of course that you make your sub available as a sex object for a gangbang.

Of course, it's particularly bad for a male sub when he's made available to men as a sex object. For a female sub, for example, it can be a male surplus with bukake at the end.

With this punishment you also have to know where the limits of your sub are and whether you might be breaking taboos.

You need: For this punishment you need a swingers club that you can visit with your sub.

Punishment 50

How about a blow training for your submissive as a punishment? Of course they practice with a dildo. The tongue should be used skillfully and deepthroat can also be a goal of this training.

You can supervise the training or let the sub do it alone. It is important that you check the result of the training at the end and check whether your sub has made any progress. Are you male yourself? Perfect. Your sub can demonstrate it to you directly and you will notice if he or she has gotten better.

Are you female Now it becomes a bit more difficult for you to control the result. You can have your sub blow your strap-on. Or if your sub is bi or a woman, you can also have a man rate their blowing skills.

You need: For this punishment you definitely need a dildo that your sub can practice with.

Punishment 51

If you don't already have it in your relationship, you can also punish your sub by having him or her wear a tag that publicly reveals him or her as your sub. Suitable for this are, for example, the ring of the O, a collar, a triskele, ...

Not everyone you meet will recognize the importance, but there will be people who will understand.

You need: For this punishment you need something to identify your sub, such as a collar.

Punishment 52

Make your sub watch porn as punishment. Not one he or she likes, of course. Is he straight through and through? How about a gay porn for him? She doesn't like gangbangs? Then you know what she needs to see.

You can control the severity of the punishment very well via the length of the porn. And if you want to be extra nasty, you can ask your sub to masturbate to this porn.

You can stick by and watch your sub or you can check on him or her every few minutes. In any case, you should check that he or she really endures his or her punishment.

You need: For this punishment you need a way to play a porn and you need a porn that your sub doesn't like.

Punishment 53

Do you like BDSM parties or have you at least thought about going to one? Then present your sub naked there. Maybe even with a collar and leash so that he or she has to follow you the whole time.

If your sub is male, you can also let him wear a chastity belt to humiliate him. Maybe you also publicly take him through with a strap-on, or let him satisfy you with a strap-on while you verbally humiliate him.

If your sub is female, you can have her do a dildo show for those present, or you can fuck her in front of everyone. If you find it horny, you can end up cumming on her face and she has to walk around with your cum on her face.

You need: A suitable BDSM or swinger party where you can also play.

Punishment 54

Another suitable punishment is that your sub is not allowed to have sex with you. He or she will have sex with an object instead. You decide whether it's the dildo, the silicone vagina or maybe the pillow or the bedpost.

But feel free to be creative. For example, strap a dildo to a teddy bear for a female sub. So feel free to come up with something.

Of course, the aim should be for your sub to have the most humiliating orgasm possible in front of your eyes.

You need: You generally do not need any special equipment for this punishment. You will surely find what you are looking for in your apartment.

Punishment 55

If you want to permanently invest in the behavior and training of your sub, send him or her to a slave training or BDSM workshop. If you search extensively on the Internet, you will surely find something suitable for your sub that could be suitable for achieving your long-term goals for your sub's training.

You need: Internet access and research options to find a suitable workshop or slave training.

Punishment 56

You want to punish your sub, but at the same time do something good for yourself? Then a visit to the thermal baths is a good way to enjoy a relaxing time.

But going to the thermal baths normally wouldn't be a punishment. You can let a male sub wear a chastity belt here while you have the key hanging around your neck. For a female sub, an anal plug would be a conceivable option.

But feel free to be creative. Maybe you can think of something you like better.

You need: For this punishment you need a thermal bath that you can visit and something to humiliate your sub there.

Punishment 57

You write a report card for your sub and you judge him or her harshly. Let him or her know what you are happy with, but focus on the areas you are unhappy with and where there is room for improvement.

Feel free to show your sub that you are disappointed in him or her. Also announce a time for a re-evaluation and let Sub know that you expect a significant improvement.

Whether you use the grading system 1-6, the point system 1-15 or another system is of course up to you.

You need: For this punishment you ideally need a computer on which you can create the certificate and a printer to print it out.

Punishment 58

Is your sub right-handed? Then, as punishment, make him or her do everything with their left hand all day. If they are left-handed, make them use their right hand, of course.

Sub will find that suddenly everything is a little more difficult. But it can also be a good exercise to increase your sub's dexterity a bit.

You need: You do not need any tools for this punishment.

Punishment 59

Sub was naughty and deserves a punishment? How about semen as a topping for dinner? Of course, if you're a male dom with a female sub, it's easy. Either you lend a hand yourself, or you let your sub lend a hand. Anyway, it all ends up on top of Sub´s meal.

Are you female, male or something else and have a male sub? Then you can combine this punishment with a ruined orgasm, for example. Or cuckolding with another man's sperm.

Now you can watch your sub as he or she tucks into a topped meal.

You need: You do not need any tools for this punishment.

Punishment 60

Do you have an open relationship or at least you are allowed to have sex with others? Then, as punishment, let your sub find someone for you to have sex with. Maybe even in front of your sub.

You need: You do not need any tools for this punishment.

Punishment 61

Your sub needs to be punished? Why not a hurdle for the sub's orgasm as punishment? From now on, and maybe for a certain time frame as well, sub has to climax you 5x, 10x, xx,... you decide... before he or she orgasms.

Of course, you can ruin that one orgasm if you want to be mean.

This is a very simple and effective way of showing your sub that you are in control of his or her lust and that he or she has to earn his or her lust first.

You need: You do not need any tools for this punishment.

Punishment 62

Go for a walk together. At a point where you might get caught, you let your sub lick you or give you a blowjob.

Believe me, your sub will go out of their way to please you quickly.

You need: You do not need any tools for this punishment.

Punishment 63

Nettles are also a nice way to punish your sub. Let sub weave a necklace out of it that he or she has to wear or how about nettles in your sub's underwear when you're out together?

Feel free to be creative with the use and let your own imagination run wild. Maybe you can think of other uses.

You need: For this punishment you need nettles.

Punishment 64

It sounds boring, but just send your sub to bed earlier as punishment. Maybe without the usual dessert, the sweets you eat in the evening or the series you are watching. Sub should calmly feel that you have the power and control.

You need: You do not need any tools for this punishment.

Punishment 65

A severe punishment, which you should also be sure if it is okay, would be if you outed your sub in front of friends and family as your sub, slave girl, slave, cuckold, ...

Let him or her wear a collar at a family celebration, for example, or casually mention in conversation that it's great that he or she is so obedient to you and you'll never again want to be without your sub, slave, cuckold , ...

You need: For this punishment you need a family celebration or a similar event.

Punishment 66

As punishment, have your sub clean your shoes until they shine properly again. It doesn't matter whether it's your elegant men's shoes or sneakers or your riding boots, patent leather pumps or dominatrix shoes. Sub should make an effort! Because you will wear these shoes at the next session.

You need: A shoe cleaning kit

Punishment 67

Go out together and now you flirt with another person in front of your sub. Do your best and work really hard so that your sub gets a little jealous.

When you are at home, however, you should take good care of your sub. There might also be hard and passionate sex if that's what you want, or just a few gentle strokes for sub.

You need: You do not need any tools for this punishment.

Punishment 68

Why should you always do all the work? As punishment, let your sub find a creative punishment for themselves. So you have given this task to him or her and he or she now has to deal with what the punishment should look like that he or she gets themself. It should, of course, be suitably tough for the offence.

If you want to make it harder for Sub, then you can directly exempt things like spanking or similar. If you're not happy with Sub's idea, have him or her come up with something else that you like better and that might be more consistent with Sub's offense. You can also threaten a penalty if Sub doesn't come up with an idea you like better.

You need: You do not need any tools for this punishment.

Punishment 69

Today, as a punishment, Sub has the task of sending you pictures of himself whenever you request it. Of course you also decide what you would like to see. Kneeling naked in front of a mirror maybe? Or a naked selfie on the balcony, in front of the window or something similar?

But you should always remember that it should also be feasible. Don't ask the sub to take pictures that he or she can't possibly take at work. So be realistic. In such a case, maybe request a nude picture from the toilet stall at the sub's work.

You need: For this punishment you need both smartphones and a messenger service with which you can send pictures.

Punishment 70

Put your sub in front of the computer and have him or her watch porn that excites him or her. Sub has to masturbate throughout the porn but is not allowed to have an orgasm.

Of course, a long porn makes this punishment harder to bear than a short porn. You should also check from time to time whether the sub is also good about masturbating and also that he or she is not just secretly having an orgasm.

There shouldn't be an orgasm. If you practice chastity, recap your sub after porn without him or her climaxing.

You need: For this punishment you need a computer with internet access.

Punishment 71

Let your sub talk to their parents, acquaintances, friends, ... during sex on the phone, while you are giving them a hand job or a blowjob or fingering, licking or spoiling them with a dildo.

Also tell him or her beforehand that he or she should try to speak normally on the phone so that no one notices.

Of course you try to elicit a lot of unpleasant noises and sounds from Sub and maybe even bring him or her to orgasm during the phone call. Let the games begin.

You need: Preferably a mobile phone from which Sub can call someone.

Punishment 72

How about a bit of exhibitionism as punishment?
Go for a walk with your sub. Of course he or she
wears socks and shoes and also a jacket or coat
that should reach to the knees.

But that's about it for clothes for your sub. The
jacket or coat is only for Sub to cover up, if
someone is coming. Otherwise Sub has to be
naked and the jacket or coat has to be worn open
when the two of you are alone and only you can
see it.

You need: For this punishment, Sub needs a jacket
or coat.

Punishment 73

As a punishment, your sub will be banned from using their cell phone all day today. Either you confiscate the cell phone or it will be locked away. Alternatively, you can also make it so that your sub has to read out every message that arrives.

You need: For this punishment you need your sub's mobile phone.

Punishment 74

You want to show your sub as punishment how good he or she has it with you as a dom and that being a dom also means work? As punishment, you switch roles for a day. Sub becomes your Dom for one day.

Today he or she has to take care of everything and also plan a BDSM session for the evening, during which he or she must of course uphold your taboos.

This will show your sub that he or she has it really good since you put a lot of work into it for him or her.

You need: You do not need any tools for this punishment.

Punishment 75

As punishment, you will ruin your sub's next 5, 10, 15... orgasms. The worse the offense, the more ruined orgasms it can be.

If you want to be cruel, then you only tell your sub after the last ruined orgasm that you punished him or her.

You need: You do not need any tools for this punishment.

Punishment 76

You always wanted to have a butler or a maid? Why not just let your sub grant that wish as punishment for an offense?

Your sub should serve you all day wearing suit or do you prefere something else? Maybe let him also wear his collar and a chastity belt?

Have you always wanted to see your sub in a maid costume? Or would you prefer sexy underwear? Just let Sub fulfill this wish.

A little tip: A bell to call your subordinate is awesome.

You need: For this punishment you need an outfit for your sub.

Punishment 77

From now on, to punish your sub, you can have him or her write a session diary in which he or she must describe each session in detail and record his or her impressions. Of course you check the diary at regular intervals and see whether your sub is also conscientiously fulfilling his or her task.

You need: For this punishment you need an empty diary or a notebook.

Punishment 78

How about some entertainment for you? Have your sub read an erotic story that you have chosen and act it out at the same time.

Is it a hard-hitting BDSM novel or is it more of a soft and chewy love story?

Anyway, it will be great fun for you to watch your sub act. And who knows, maybe you'll get a taste for it and this punishment is more common now.

You need: An erotic story of your choice.

Punishment 79

As a punishment, it can sometimes be something really nasty. Especially if your sub really deserves it. Give your sub a time limit to have an orgasm. Give him or her 30 seconds, 60 seconds...you know your sub best. Choose a time window that is as close as possible to the time it would take your sub to have an orgasm.

Your goal, of course, is for the sub to stop just before he or she gets there. But let him or her have the orgasm if you chose the wrong time slot. After all, your sub can't do anything about it.

You need: For this punishment you need a stopwatch or a timer. You can use the timer from your phone, which is the easiest option.

Punishment 80

As punishment, give your sub the task of writing down his or her dream session. It's a nice activity for your sub and of course it could be quite interesting for you too.

You can pick up the text your sub wrote and surprise or reward your sub with this session. However, Sub has to earn it first.

You need: For this punishment you need something to write.

Punishment 81

You want to punish and humiliate your sub? Put bells on her nipples or his penis and demand that you don't want to hear a sound.

Each ring means a hit with the whip, the paddle, the cane, ... whichever you prefer.

The best part is that if Sub moves at the smack that there is for ringing, there will most likely be a ringing sound again because your sub will certainly not be staying completely still. This means that the next shot can take place immediately.

You need: For this punishment you need bells that you can attach to the breasts or penis and a percussion instrument of your choice.

Punishment 82

For punishment, have your sub ask other people how he or she should be punished online. You can then take the best ideas presented to you by your sub and use them directly. Make a note of the other suggestions if there was something you particularly liked. This way you can use these ideas as punishment for your sub at a later date.

You need: For this punishment, your sub needs internet access.

Punishment 83

As punishment you cum on your sub's face or make your sub cum on his own face. Now comes the real punishment. You go for a walk together, but your sub is not allowed to wash the cum off their face and has to go outside with you. Only when you are back from your walk you allow your sub to wash their face.

You need: You do not need any tools for this punishment.

Punishment 84

Do you and your sub often play X-Box, Playstation or something similar together? Have your sub play with the controller behind their back as punishment.

It is best to choose a game in which you compete against each other. Now your sub has a really great playing handicap and you have a huge advantage. Hopefully he or she doesn't win anyway. That would be really embarrassing for you.

You need: For this punishment you need a game console with controllers.

Punishment 85

As punishment, have your sub openly carry a sex toy around with them all day. Does he or she have to hold a dildo in their hand when going for a walk or is the butt plug worn around the neck like a pendant? You decide. It will definitely get embarrassing for your sub to be out in public like this.

You need: For this punishment you need a sex toy that your sub can wear openly.

Punishment 86

Let it get a little romantic and have Sub write you a love letter as punishment. On beautiful paper, of course, handwritten and in calligraphy. After all, you want to be able to enjoy the letter and certainly want to keep it when you get it.

You need: For this punishment you need stationery and something to write with.

Punishment 87

As punishment, encourage your sub's artistic talents and have him or her draw what they want you to do in the next session. Of course, this punishment is especially great if your sub can't draw well and you can make fun of their pathetic efforts.

Maybe you don't even recognize what Sub is imagining and wanting to show you. Feel free to comment on the drawings. Especially if they're drawn really badly.

You need: For this punishment you need something with which and on which your sub can draw.

Punishment 88

Would you like to humiliate your sub as a punishment? Just have him or her wear a pacifier instead of a gag to keep him or her quiet.

Comments such as "Bad children just get the pacifier to keep them quiet" can also have a very nice effect.

Feel free to describe what your sub looks like to you with the pacifier in their mouth. Like a giant baby maybe?

You need: For this punishment you need a pacifier.

Punishment 89

Today, as punishment, your sub is the plate on which the food is beautifully presented for you and your visiting friends.

Of course Sub has to wash herself properly beforehand and then lay naked on the table and you spread the food nice and handsome on her or his body.

Cover all the important spots. The more eaten, the more your sub will be exposed.

You need: For this punishment you need a dining table that is large enough to support the weight of your sub.

Punishment 90

Your sub is not one of the foot fetishists? Still, it's an idea that he or she massages your feet as punishment. Kisses are of course also possible, as long as your sub doesn't dislike it.

Banish your sub to where he or she belongs for a while. Namely kneeling at your feet and busy massaging them extensively.

You need: You do not need any tools for this punishment.

Punishment 91

As punishment, you go to a sex shop together and look for something humiliating for the sub. The best way is for other customers to notice.

You might even ask another customer for their opinion on whether what you have selected is really suitable for your sub.

When paying at the cash register, you make it clear that it is for your sub and not for you.

You need: For this punishment you need a sex shop that you can visit.

Punishment 92

How about letting your sub do your manicure as punishment? And of course he or she has to make an effort to please you. Otherwise, of course, you can also let yourself be licked while you take care of your manicure yourself if you don't trust him.

The male dom will certainly find more pleasure in being bathed and pampered by the sub. You can let sub wash your hair and of course sub has to dry you off and blow dry your hair.

You need: You do not need any tools for this punishment.

Punishment 93

As a punishment, you can also offer your sub on the internet. Whether you then really make him or her available is of course up to you.

But wouldn't it be interesting to see how much interest there is in your sub?

You need: For this punishment you need the internet.

Punishment 94

The following punishment is more appropriate for a female dom with a male sub. If you're a male dom who likes anal with yourself, this punishment might be something for you too.

Your sub puts on a strap-on to pleasure you. Especially with male subs, it's great that you can use a dildo that's bigger than their penis, which has a very strong psychological effect and you might also lock his cock in a chastity belt.

Also, as a male dom, you may have some ideas that will make it more humiliating for your sub to perform this punishment.

You need: For this punishment you definitely need a strap-on dildo.

Punishment 95

Pet play is actually always a good punishment. Your sub is your pet for a whole day. Of course, the time can also be different if a day is too long for you. Then just a few hours.

How about a dog or a cat? There are even butt plugs with animal tails if that's how you'd like to see your sub.

Maybe you even take your sub for a walk and take him or her out for a bit. In any case, Sub is only allowed to make animal sounds and must move like the chosen animal until the penalty is over.

You need: You do not need any tools for this punishment.

Punishment 96

Send your sub shopping and have him or her buy a box of condoms and a single banana or cucumber. nothing else. Just these two items.

It's going to be quite embarrassing at the checkout if there's nothing else on the line aside from these items.

You need: You do not need any tools for this punishment.

Punishment 97

How about a punishment with an erotic photo shoot, where you mainly take humiliating pictures of your sub? She with dildos in vagina and anus or he in the chastity belt while riding a dildo, for example. But these are just examples. Surely you always had something in mind about what kind of photo you would like to have of your sub. Use the penalty to finally get this picture now.

You need: For this punishment you need a photo camera or a mobile phone camera.

Punishment 98

Sub was naughty? That won't happen again anytime soon! For a whole day, he or she is only allowed to communicate with sounds and noises, but not with language.

Be curious what noises you might hear from your sub.

You need: You do not need any tools for this punishment.

Punishment 99

You always wanted to shoot your own porn? Then do it as punishment for your sub. Whether you wear masks, whether your faces can be seen, of course you have to know what is possible. Also the subject matter and whether there is a script, whether you just set up a camera and press rec, or whether someone plays cameraman for you are all aspects to consider.

And of course you should also decide what to do with the video. Should it maybe be uploaded to the internet? What happens to the video if you and your sub break up?

You need: For this punishment you need a video camera.

Punishment 100

As the 100th punishment, I just want to appeal to your creativity. A punishment can gain meaning if it's something personal and something that you've created especially for the two of you.

With the 99 previous penalties I think you have a good starting point to let your imagination run wild and find your own good penalties or maybe combine some of mine.

Afterword

Now all I have to do is thank you for reading my book to the end and I hope you enjoyed it and that you might have found one or the other idea that you will implement with your sub.

I would appreciate if you write a review if the book was helpful to you. I know that not all punishments have been for you, but there was certainly something for you.

I would also be happy if you keep your eyes open for other books by me. I plan to publish more books about BDSM in the future.

Stay perverted and open to new things

Dom. Ination

Impressum: Stefan Schäfer, Lindenstraße 19, 61279 Grävenwiesbach, Deutschland

Made in United States
Orlando, FL
18 July 2023

35251043R00059